Silhouettes in the Twilight Hollow

In the glow of fading light,
Shadows dance, soft and bright.
Whispers float through the trees,
Echoes carried by the breeze.

Misty figures intertwine,
Lost in stories, so divine.
The stars peek through the night,
Glimmers of forgotten sight.

Every silhouette a tale,
Of times when hope would prevail.
A secret world now unveiled,
In twilight's grip, dreams are sailed.

Rustling Secrets on the Weathered Planks

Beneath the old, creaking wood,
Lies a path where dreams once stood.
Whispers of the past resound,
In every corner, truths are found.

Leaves on the ground gently sigh,
As stories twist and flit by.
The rhythm of time, soft yet clear,
Echoes of memories, so near.

Footfalls linger, stories awake,
Hidden treasures, hearts at stake.
Listen close to the rustling song,
Where secrets of the planks belong.

A Serenade to the Winged Wanderers

High above, they soar and glide,
Freedom found in every stride.
Feathers whisper in the air,
Nature's chorus, wild and rare.

Through the valleys, over the hills,
A symphony of soaring thrills.
Each note a journey, bold and grand,
A dance of life, by fate's own hand.

From dusk to dawn, their songs take flight,
In harmony with the fading light.
Adventurers on a boundless spree,
The winged wanderers roam so free.

Pine Needles and Talon Traces

Amidst the pines, the ground is strewn,
With needles that cradle the moon.
A tapestry of nature's grace,
Where beasts leave their silent trace.

Talon marks upon the earth,
Tell of stories, pain, and birth.
In quiet woods, their journeys blend,
With secrets that nature tends.

Whispers linger in the air,
Tales of life, both wild and rare.
In the shadows, the stories thrive,
Pine needles guard where spirits strive.

Embracing the Sky's Soft Embrace

In twilight's hush, the stars awake,
A gentle breeze begins to break.
Whispers of night, sweet and low,
Each twinkle beckons, soft and slow.

Clouds dance lightly, dreams take flight,
Kissed by the glow of silver light.
Nature sings in a calming sigh,
As we embrace the vast, wide sky.

Hearts align with the moon's soft grace,
In this still moment, we find our place.
Boundless skies overhead so bright,
In tender warmth, we feel the night.

Where Feathered Friends Greet the Day

Morning light through branches weaves,
Chirps and whistles paint the leaves.
With wings unfurled, they greet the dawn,
A symphony of life reborn.

Softly glowing in the sun's embrace,
Feathered friends in joyful chase.
They flit and flutter, bright and free,
In harmony, they sing with glee.

With every note, they share delight,
In this warm and golden light.
Nature welcomes, pure and true,
Where feathered hearts find joy anew.

Comforts of Wood, Sky, and Flight

Beneath the trees, I find my peace,
Where gentle whispers never cease.
The scent of pine and earth collide,
In nature's arms, my heart will bide.

High above, the canvas gleams,
Blue and vast, a realm of dreams.
Wings take off, they kiss the air,
In flight, they shed away all care.

Balancing on the edge of land,
With roots in soil and dreams so grand.
Each flutter speaks of joy and hope,
In nature's cradle, we learn to cope.

Rising and Falling with the Breeze

The sun ascends, we lift our gaze,
Waves of warmth in morning's haze.
Leaves are dancing, gentle sway,
A chorus sings of brand new day.

Kites soar high in endless blue,
With every gust, they gain their cue.
Floating freely, no weight to bind,
In this moment, peace we find.

As daylight wanes and shadows grow,
We drift like clouds, moving slow.
In twilight's arms, we learn to glide,
Rising and falling, side by side.

The Stillness Before the Next Flight

In the calm of dusk's embrace,
Wings prepare for the race.
Soft whispers of the night,
Hover close, just out of sight.

Clouds gather with a sigh,
Promises of journeys high.
A moment stretched in time,
As dreams begin to climb.

The engines hum a tune,
Underneath the rising moon.
Passengers gaze in thought,
Of places life has brought.

Silence cloaks the tarmac wide,
While the heartbeats slowly bide.
Eager souls await their turn,
For the skies their hopes to earn.

Through the stillness, hearts ignite,
Ready for the hopeful flight.
With a gentle breeze at hand,
They embrace the promised land.

Nature's Tapestry Among Starlit Pines

Beneath the whispers of the trees,
Nature weaves with gentle ease.
Stars adorn the velvet night,
In their glow, the world feels right.

Crickets sing a lullaby,
As the moon watches from on high.
The scent of pine in the air,
Fills the heart with tranquil care.

Roots entwined with ancient lore,
Every path leads to more.
Creatures dance in shadows deep,
In the woods, the secrets keep.

Meadows bloom with colors bright,
Underneath the starry light.
Each moment feels divine,
A tapestry by design.

As dawn nudges night away,
Nature shares another day.
In the stillness, peace defines,
Life's beauty among the pines.

The Watcher's Lodge: A Rustic Album

In the lodge of timber grand,
Stories linger, hand in hand.
Photographs of days gone by,
Smile from frames, oh how they lie.

Each corner holds a tale unspooled,
Moments captured, carefully schooled.
With the crackle of the fire,
Legends born of youthful desire.

Beneath the eaves, the shadows dance,
Echoes of a fleeting chance.
Memories like autumn leaves,
Whisper softly, as the heart believes.

Candles flicker, casting light,
On recollections, bold and bright.
A rustic charm that gently calls,
To the heart, through these weathered walls.

In every timber, every grain,
Lives a struggle, joy, and pain.
The lodge stands tall, a guardian bold,
Of stories woven, timeless and old.

Nature's Artwork on Rustic Railings

Twisted vines cling to wood,
With blossoms bright and wild,
Nature's brush paints the scene,
Each detail sweet and mild.

Rust and green embrace the posts,
A tapestry unfolds,
Whispers of the summer breeze,
In colors rich and bold.

Birds dance lightly on the rails,
Their songs a soft delight,
Sunset drips its golden hue,
As day turns into night.

In this space, the world is still,
Artistry of the land,
Rustic charm captures hearts,
By gentle nature's hand.

So linger here and breathe it in,
Each moment feels so grand,
Nature's artwork on rustic rails,
A peaceful, sacred land.

Where Pines Whisper to the Sky

Tall and proud, the pines do stand,
Their needles swaying free,
Whispers float on gentle winds,
Between earth and sky's decree.

A symphony of rustling leaves,
Nature's lullaby, it sings,
Echoes dance in twilight's glow,
With secrets that the forest brings.

Misty mornings greet the dawn,
Sunlight filters through,
Golden rays on emerald tips,
Softened by the dew.

In this realm where shadows play,
And dreams take gentle flight,
The pines hold stories yet untold,
In the hush of fading light.

So walk beneath their sprawling boughs,
And let your spirit soar,
For where pines whisper to the sky,
You'll find your heart restore.

A Home Among the Green Canopy

Underneath the leafy roof,
A sanctuary waits,
Sunbeams dance on forest floor,
While nature celebrates.

Mossy stones and winding paths,
Entwined with roots so old,
Tell tales of a timeless world,
In whispers soft and bold.

The songs of birds become the breeze,
A choir in the air,
While butterflies in colors bright,
Float gently without care.

This vibrant life enchants the soul,
With magic all around,
A home among the green canopy,
Where tranquility is found.

So take a moment, breathe it in,
Let nature's love embrace,
In the heart of verdant woods,
You'll find your sacred space.

Silhouettes of the Faithful Hunter

As twilight falls, the shadows stretch,
In silence, they await,
A silhouette against the dusk,
With purpose, strong and great.

Eyes keen and heart attuned,
To rhythms of the night,
In nature's cloak, the hunter moves,
With grace and fears set right.

Tracking paths of ancient trails,
Among the trees he roams,
The whispers of the wilderness,
Guide him safely home.

Each heartbeat syncs with nature's pulse,
A dance of life defined,
In stillness comes the hunter's grace,
As instincts intertwined.

So marvel at this noble art,
Of balance, skill, and fate,
In silhouettes of faithful ones,
Reside the stories great.

Shadows of Grace Amongst the Pines

Under the tall and whispering trees,
Shadow dances, a gentle tease.
Graceful forms in the muted light,
Nature's art, a tranquil sight.

Beneath the canopy, deep and wide,
Secrets of the forest bide.
Leaves murmur with a soft embrace,
As time pauses in this sacred space.

The scent of needles fills the air,
In this haven, free from care.
Every rustle tells a tale,
Carried softly on the gale.

Roots entwined, the ground does sigh,
As branches stretch to the vast sky.
In silence, wisdom finds its place,
In shadows deep, we find our grace.

Yet as the sun begins to set,
This enchanted realm we won't forget.
A memory etched in every heart,
In whispers of the woods, we start.

Breezes Carrying Feathered Whispers

Through the trees, the breezes roam,
Carrying whispers, nature's home.
Feathers flutter on the wind,
A dance of life where dreams begin.

Songs of birds in melodious flight,
Echo gently, a pure delight.
Each note a story, softly told,
In the arms of the trees, we behold.

Gliding gracefully, they soar high,
Painting patterns across the sky.
A symphony in each fleeting sound,
In harmony, the earth is crowned.

Among the branches, secrets weave,
In this place, hearts dare to believe.
Every breeze a gentle caress,
Nature's lullaby, purest bliss.

With every sigh, new dreams are spun,
Under the warmth of the setting sun.
Feathered whispers in twilight's grace,
Forever linger in this sacred space.

The Enchanted Sorcery of the Arbor

In the depths of the ancient trees,
Sorcery dances in the breeze.
Whispers of magic, soft and slow,
In the heart of the forest, secrets flow.

Twilight casts a spell so deep,
Inviting all the dreams to leap.
With each shadow that starts to play,
The world around begins to sway.

Mossy carpets beneath our feet,
In every corner, wonders meet.
A flicker here, a shimmer there,
The enchantment fills the twilight air.

Roots entangle like heartstrings tight,
Binding souls in the soft moonlight.
Here stories weave through every bough,
In the enchanted, we find our vow.

As the night unfolds its tender cloak,
In hushed tones, ancient oaks spoke.
With every rustling leaf and sigh,
We're reminded of magic, you and I.

Harmony in the Canopy's Hold

High above where the eagles glide,
Harmony in the branches resides.
Leaves intertwine in a delicate dance,
A celebration of nature's chance.

With sunlight streaming through the green,
A canvas painted, rarely seen.
Each leaf a note, each breeze a song,
In the canopy, we all belong.

Gentle creatures stir and play,
In this realm where shadows stay.
Their laughter echoes, soft and sweet,
A symphony where spirits meet.

Underneath the twilight's glow,
The world whispers secrets only it knows.
In the harmony of the trees,
Lies the magic of the gentle breeze.

Together we find a tranquil heart,
In the forest's embrace, we'll never part.
In unity, we rise and unfold,
A story of life, in the trees told.

Winged Messengers of the Conifer

In the shade of ancient pines,
Whispers of the wind divine.
Feathered creatures take their flight,
Carving paths in morning light.

Branches sway with softest grace,
Nature's calm, a sacred space.
Beaks so bright, a vivid hue,
Tell the tales of skies so blue.

Songs of joy fill azure air,
Echoes drifting without a care.
Busy wings like fleeting dreams,
Dancing through the sunlit beams.

Amidst the needles, secrets lie,
Underneath the sprawling sky.
Messengers from realms of green,
Bringing stories yet unseen.

In the dusk, their shadows blend,
As day and night begin to mend.
In every chirp, a soft farewell,
To the tales the trees could tell.

Sunlit Moments in Feathered Flight

Beneath the canopy of gold,
Moments whisper, tales unfold.
Wings aflutter, hearts take wing,
In the sun, the songbirds sing.

A dance of shadows on the ground,
As laughter of the birds resound.
Each heartbeat echoes in the air,
A fleeting joy, a light to share.

In glimmers bright, they take their grace,
A fleeting brush, a soft embrace.
Golden rays on feathered bliss,
In every flutter, nature's kiss.

Through emerald leaves, they weave and glide,
In sunlit moments, they confide.
In harmony, their voices blend,
A melody without an end.

As twilight falls, they slowly fade,
In memories, their songs portrayed.
Each moment steeped in gentle light,
In feathered flight, pure delight.

Nature's Palette on Verdant Canvas

The colors bloom where silence dwells,
In gentle strokes, harmony swells.
Greens and blues in soft embrace,
Nature's art, a sacred space.

Petals open, bright and bold,
Stories of the earth retold.
With every brush of sunlit kiss,
A touch of joy, a moment's bliss.

Birdsongs weave through vibrant air,
Echoing their beauty rare.
Each feather, each leaf, a tale,
In nature's heart, they softly sail.

The canvas breathes with life anew,
A masterpiece in every hue.
In wild embrace, colors collide,
In nature's dance, we shall abide.

So pause awhile and breathe it in,
Where every color speaks within.
A tapestry of life, divine,
On verdant canvas, hearts entwine.

Twilight Revelry of the Feathered Seraphs

As day retreats, a soft parade,
Of feathered beings, unafraid.
In twilight's glow, they softly play,
Chasing dusk, the fading day.

Wings aglow with ember's light,
Seraphs dance through coming night.
Whispers low, a joyful sound,
In the stillness, peace is found.

Silhouettes against the sky,
Softly gliding, soaring high.
Their laughter mingles with the breeze,
Bringing solace, hearts at ease.

With every flap, a story told,
Of love and dreams, both brave and bold.
In the twilight, beauty lies,
In the dance of the glowing skies.

As stars emerge, they take their flight,
In the embrace of coming night.
Feathered seraphs, wild and free,
In twilight's revelry, we see.

Hunger of the Skybound Soul

Above the earth, the eagles soar,
Yearning hearts reach for more.
Clouds whisper dreams to the brave,
In the winds, our spirits crave.

Stars are beacons in the night,
Guiding us with their soft light.
Find the courage to ascend,
Let the sky be your friend.

Mountains call with silent grace,
Chasing freedom in this space.
With every breath, we ignite,
The hunger felt deep in flight.

In vast horizons, we reside,
With hopes and wishes as our guide.
As we reach for skies so high,
Embrace the hunger, let it fly.

A symphony of dreams takes wing,
In every heartbeat, wild thoughts sing.
For the skybound soul must roam,
Finding solace, creating home.

A Dance Between Earth and Sky

Beneath the sun, the fields awake,
In rhythm with every quake.
The breeze carries whispers light,
Dancing freely, pure delight.

Clouds cavort in pastel hues,
As nature shares her vibrant views.
Grass sways gently, hands in prayer,
A harmony found in the air.

Raindrops play like gentle drums,
Echoes of life, the heartbeat hums.
Through petals soft, the earth replies,
In this dance, the spirit flies.

Mountains rise, a grand ballet,
As shadows lengthen, night comes to play.
The stars twirl in cosmic glee,
Uniting both land and sea.

Each twilight whispers secrets old,
Of stories shared and dreams retold.
In this dance, we find our way,
Between the earth and skies so gray.

The Porch that Knew Their Flight

On a porch with weathered wood,
They carved their dreams as best they could.
Laughter echoed in the air,
Moments frozen, hearts laid bare.

As sunsets kissed the day goodbye,
They watched the robins learn to fly.
Each wingbeat spoke of journeys near,
The promise of the skies to cheer.

Seasons shifted, time did glide,
Yet on that porch, love would abide.
A witness to the tales of grace,
And every joy that life embraced.

When storms would chase the sun away,
The porch would cradle hopes at bay.
Through whispers soft, the memories blend,
Of wanderers who love transcend.

Now vacant chairs, with echoes hold,
The warmth of stories yet untold.
In stillness lingers all their flight,
A porch alive with love's pure light.

Rustic Reflections of Nature's Kindness

In the hush of morning's glow,
Nature's kindness starts to show.
Birdsong breaks the silent dawn,
Welcoming dreams to linger on.

Fields of gold stretch far and wide,
Gentle hills, a peaceful tide.
Every tree a witness stands,
Holding tales of quiet lands.

The brook sings soft through rocks and roots,
Sharing secrets as it hoots.
Wildflowers dance in gentle breeze,
Whispering life, causing hearts to ease.

Beneath the shade, the earth confides,
The laughter of the stream abides.
With every rustle, nature speaks,
In humble ways, her kindness leaks.

When skies unfold with colors bright,
And shadows melt in fading light,
We find reflections of our souls,
In rustic charms, where nature consoles.

Threads of Gold Beneath the Branches

In dappled light, the whispers weave,
Golden threads through leaves that breathe.
Each flicker captured in a dance,
Nature's magic, a fleeting chance.

Beneath the boughs, where secrets lie,
Scattered dreams float up to sky.
The gentle rustle sings of grace,
A tapestry in this sacred place.

Sunbeams trickle through the green,
Glimmers soft, like silk unseen.
They stitch together dusk and dawn,
In a world where shadows are drawn.

From roots entwined, the stories flow,
In every breeze, their voices grow.
Embroidered tales of times gone by,
Eternity weaves as spirits fly.

The golden threads in nature's fold,
Whisper truths silently told.
In the heart of every tree,
A world awaits for you and me.

Guardians of the Coastal Pines

Standing tall, they face the sea,
Guardians of the land, wild and free.
With arms stretched wide, they catch the breeze,
Whispering secrets among the trees.

Their needles dance in salty air,
A watchful presence, always there.
Each storm that rages, they withstand,
Anchored deep in shifting sand.

Crimson sunsets paint their crowns,
As evening whispers through sleepy towns.
Beneath the stars, they softly sway,
Holding shadows of night at bay.

In their embrace, a spirit thrives,
Carving paths where the ocean dives.
They cradle dreams along the shore,
Lifetimes etched in tales of yore.

The coastal pines, steadfast and bold,
Each ring of bark, a story told.
In their kinship with wind and tide,
A legacy we cannot hide.

The Poet's Refuge: A Feathered Pace

In quiet glades where soft winds sigh,
A poet wanders, thoughts go high.
With every step, the world awakes,
As feathered dreams in silence make.

Beneath the boughs, a sacred space,
Words like whispers find their place.
In every rustle, a thought takes flight,
A gentle muse in the fading light.

With ink and feather, tales are spun,
Of moonlit nights and days undone.
The heart transforms as verses flow,
A river of words, both high and low.

Each bird that calls, a stanza sung,
Nature's music, forever young.
In stillness rests a world so vast,
Moments captured, shadows cast.

The poet's refuge, a sacred pace,
In every sigh, a warm embrace.
Feathers drift on whispering breeze,
Where words unfurl, the heart finds ease.

Rustic Reflections in Feather and Wood

In aged woods, the stories dwell,
Each grain a whisper, each knot a spell.
Reflections dance on surfaces worn,
Echoes of life, a spirit reborn.

The rustic charm of feathered flight,
Captures dreams in fading light.
Each brush of wings across the air,
Brings tales of wonder, light as air.

Old timber creaks with wisdom shared,
In quiet moments, nothing's spared.
Nature's canvas in hues so true,
Each color sings in morning dew.

The harmony of wings and boughs,
In tranquil corners, the heart allows.
To linger long in soft embrace,
As time dissolves in this sacred space.

Rustic reflections, sighs of wood,
Breath of life in the quiet flood.
A perfect union, feather and tree,
In every heartbeat, a melody.

Echoes Between the Pine Trees

Whispers float on the gentle breeze,
Secrets held by the swaying leaves.
Footsteps soft on the forest floor,
Echoes linger, forever more.

Sunlight dapples, a golden hue,
Birds take flight, in skies so blue.
Nature sings in a tranquil tune,
Underneath the watchful moon.

Branches stretch, and shadows play,
Time stands still at the end of day.
Memories dance, like flickering light,
In the embrace of the falling night.

Ferns unfurl in the cool damp earth,
Quiet moments, a time of rebirth.
Each heartbeat echoes with the pine,
In the sanctuary, so divine.

Voices linger in the twilight glow,
With every breeze, they ebb and flow.
Life unfolds in its purest form,
Within the pines, where dreams are born.

Beneath the Canopy's Embrace

Beneath the leaves, a world unfolds,
Stories whispered in greens and golds.
Roots entwined in a rich embrace,
Nature's wonders, a sacred space.

Sunlight filters, warm and bright,
Creating patterns of sheer delight.
Soft rustles stir the quiet air,
Life awakens in everywhere.

Moss carpets the ground in a soft bed,
Tiny creatures make their way ahead.
The canopy hums a sweet refrain,
A melody born from the gentle rain.

Twilight falls, with colors bold,
Stories of dusk, beautifully told.
Hidden in shadows, magic thrives,
In this haven, where nature thrives.

Stars peek through the leafy veil,
Guiding hearts, on paths they trail.
A symphony of life, night ignites,
In the canopy's embrace, pure delights.

Heartbeats of the Lithe Sky Dancers

In the meadow, bodies sway,
With each breath, they steal away.
Whirling spirits spin and glide,
In the dance of life, they abide.

Joy erupts like fireflies bright,
Illuminating the tranquil night.
With hearts that beat to the rhythm's call,
Together they rise, never to fall.

Soft whispers carry through the air,
Each movement speaks of love and care.
Under the watchful, gleaming stars,
They paint the sky with vibrant scars.

Moonlight wraps them in a soft hug,
As shadows play, and spirits tug.
Every heartbeat, a pulse divine,
In the chorus of the night, they shine.

Lithe and free, they roam so wide,
In endless dance, they confide.
The world their stage, a grand display,
In transient forms, they fade away.

A Tapestry Woven in Woodland Colors

In the forest where hues collide,
Colors weave, side by side.
Crimson leaves and azure skies,
Nature's palette, a sweet surprise.

Golden rays through branches stream,
Creating light in a vibrant dream.
Emerald moss carpets the ground,
A tapestry of life, all around.

Rustling ferns in delicate greens,
Whisper secrets of tranquil scenes.
Every petal a brushstroke rare,
An artwork crafted with love and care.

Seasons shift, with grace and poise,
Painting pathways, a song that joys.
Each moment cherished, a fleeting brush,
In woodland colors, there lies a hush.

As twilight settles, hues intertwine,
The forest breathes, a sacred shrine.
In this realm of boundless art,
A tapestry wove, forever in heart.

The Gentle Brush of Nature's Ink

In whispering woods, where shadows play,
Each leaf a page, come what may.
The sun spills gold on emerald hues,
Nature paints life, her wondrous muse.

A brook hums low, a gentle tune,
With every ripple, it sheds a rune.
Mountains stand tall, with stories to share,
In the vast canvas of open air.

Breezes dance through branches wide,
Carrying whispers of the tide.
Flowers bloom in colors bright,
Nature's ink, a pure delight.

With every sunrise, the world awakes,
In stunning strokes, the artist makes.
Creatures wander, roam, and scurry,
In the beauty, there's no hurry.

So let us pause and breathe it in,
The gentle brush, where dreams begin.
In quiet moments, find your way,
In Nature's ink, forever stay.

Songs of the Roaming Spirits

In valleys deep, where echoes roam,
The spirits sing of their lost home.
With every note, the shadows flow,
A melody, both soft and low.

The wind it carries tales of old,
Of adventures brave, and hearts bold.
Through ancient trees, their whispers weave,
In songs of joy, we believe.

Stars ignite the velvet night,
Guiding souls with shimmering light.
From mountain heights to ocean's grace,
The spirits gather, a timeless embrace.

With drums of thunder, the heartbeat starts,
Connecting us all, as nature imparts.
In reverberating echoes clear,
The songs of spirits we hold dear.

So listen close, let your heart soar,
For they sing of life, forevermore.
In every whisper, a spark ignites,
In songs of spirits, our souls take flight.

Reflections in a Skyward Glade

In a glade where the daylight spills,
Mirrored skies on tranquil frills.
Dancing clouds with shadows cast,
Time stands still, forever past.

The trees, they stretch with all their might,
Reaching high in the fading light.
Reflecting dreams on silver streams,
In nature's realm, we find our themes.

Butterflies flit with gentle grace,
Painting stories all over the place.
In silence speaks the heart divine,
In this glade, our spirits align.

The sun dips low, a fiery hue,
As twilight covers the earth anew.
In shadowed folds, the night unfolds,
The glade breathes secrets, yet untold.

So come and wander, free your mind,
In reflections, true beauty find.
In the skyward glade, we shall stay,
Where dreams and nature dance and play.

The Lullaby of the Open Air

Underneath the vast, starry sky,
The world whispers a soft good-bye.
With every rustle, a soothing char,
The open air sings from afar.

Moonlight drapes in silver threads,
Cradling all in sleepy beds.
Winds weave tales of peace and rest,
In nature's heart, we are blessed.

Crickets chirp in rhythmic time,
Their lullabies a gentle rhyme.
Fireflies spark a brilliant dance,
The night invites us to take a chance.

As branches sway with a tender moan,
We find comfort, never alone.
Nature's chorus wraps us tight,
Guiding souls into the night.

So close your eyes, let worries flee,
In the embrace of tranquility.
The open air will always care,
With lullabies, forever there.

The Language of Feather and Branch

In whispers soft, the branches sway,
The feathered friends dance in the day.
Songs of the leaves, a gentle hum,
A tale of life, where joy is from.

Beneath the sky, both blue and wide,
Nestled secrets that nature hides.
Each flutter speaks a hidden lore,
In every breath, the wilds explore.

The rustling sounds invite a pause,
In silence deep, we find our cause.
To listen close, to see the spark,
Where life unfolds from light to dark.

Feathers drift on a soft, warm breeze,
Among the branches, it's time to please.
The dance continues, a sacred rite,
In harmony, we take our flight.

Together we weave, a story spun,
With nature's grace, we are all one.
In every note, a bond we seek,
The language found, our hearts will speak.

Porches Adorned with Nature's Gifts

The porch adorned with blooms so bright,
Nature's gifts come into sight.
Petals dance with the morning sun,
Whispers of joy for everyone.

Wooden beams embrace with care,
Breezes carry scents through the air.
A place to pause, to laugh and dream,
Where life flows in a gentle stream.

Little critters scurry near,
A garden alive, a refuge dear.
Children's laughter fills the days,
As sunlight weaves through leafy ways.

Time slows down on this cherished space,
With nature's charm, a warm embrace.
Each moment shared, a treasure found,
In this refuge, love abounds.

As twilight falls and shadows play,
We gather close, as night turns day.
In every heartbeat, the story lives,
Porches adorned, where nature gives.

Echoes Echoed Among the Pines

Among the pines, where shadows dwell,
Echoes linger, a timeless spell.
Whispers of wind through needles pass,
Tales of the woods in soft, green grass.

The bark holds stories, old and wise,
While sunbeams dance, a sweet surprise.
Rustling leaves, a symphonic call,
In nature's theater, we are all.

Each footfall speaks of paths once trod,
In dreams of forest, we find a nod.
The pines, they sway, in rhythm slow,
A heartbeat shared, a tranquil flow.

As twilight whispers, the day retreats,
The echoes fade, as silence greets.
Yet in the stillness, life prevails,
Among the pines, the heart exhales.

Together still, we share the night,
In moonlit grace, our spirits take flight.
As dawn awakens, the echoes bloom,
Among the pines, we find our room.

Whims of the Winds at Twilight

The winds at twilight begin to play,
With secrets carried from far away.
A soft caress, a gentle sigh,
As day bids night a sweet goodbye.

Whims of whispers weave through the air,
Stories unfurl, for those who care.
Laughter mingles with the fading light,
A symphony born of day and night.

The stars peek through, a shy debut,
While shadows dance, embracing the hue.
Each breeze tells tales of what has been,
Adventures dwelled in the spaces between.

As twilight deepens, hearts will soar,
In the winds, we find so much more.
Nature's chorus sings out loud,
As night unfolds beneath its shroud.

In every gust, a promise sweet,
Of dreams and journeys soon to meet.
We gather close, as lanterns glow,
In whims of the winds, our spirits flow.

The Sparrow's Friend at Dusk

In the fading light, shadows creep,
The sparrow sings as the world drifts to sleep.
A friend by the nest, with watchful eyes,
Whispers of secrets under twilight skies.

Leaves rustle softly, a lullaby's tune,
As stars awaken, brightening soon.
The promise of dawn in the fading glow,
A bond that in silence continues to grow.

The gentle breeze carries tales from afar,
Of journeys taken beneath the evening star.
Together they share this tranquil embrace,
Finding solace and peace, in this sacred space.

With each sun's decline, their friendship anew,
In whispers of dusk, a world made for two.
The chirps intertwine, melody sweet,
As night wraps them close, where dreams gently meet.

So here in the twilight, their hearts are aligned,
Nature's soft canvas, in magic designed.
The sparrow and friend, beneath the same sky,
In the hush of the dusk, together they fly.

Rustic Hues and Soaring Views

Golden fields glisten under a warm sun,
Rustic hues painted, a day that's begun.
Crisp air embraces, with whispers of grain,
Nature's soft palette, free from all pain.

Mountains stand tall, a canvas of green,
Soaring views open, a sight so serene.
Clouds drift slowly, like thoughts on the breeze,
In this vibrant moment, the soul finds its ease.

Horizon stretches far, where earth meets the sky,
Birds dance above, in a grand waltz they fly.
Rustling leaves echo, life's sweet refrain,
A melody found in this earthly domain.

Every color tells a story untold,
In the heart of the land, brave and bold.
The sun dips low, casting shadows anew,
Rustic hues blending in twilight's soft dew.

As stars soon appear, the day's dreams unfold,
In whispers of night, new journeys are told.
From rustic beginnings to views up above,
Nature wraps all in a blanket of love.

Thoughts on the Wind's Gentle Breath

Whispers of wind, a soft serenade,
Carrying thoughts where memories fade.
Through fields of wildflowers, free as can be,
Nature's soft breath sings its own melody.

Every rustle of leaves, a story it shares,
Echoes of laughter, of dreams and of cares.
It dances through valleys, over hillsides grand,
Reminding us gently of life's loving hand.

Clouds drift lazily, casting shades below,
In the warmth of the sun, a soft golden glow.
Thoughts take flight, like birds in the clear,
In the arms of the wind, there's nothing to fear.

Moments suspended, in stillness they stay,
The wind's gentle breath leads us on our way.
Through whispers of twilight and dawn's early light,
It guides our reflections into the night.

In the heart of the breeze, truths softly unfurl,
A connection that deepens, transcending this world.
With thoughts on the wind, we find strength anew,
In the gentle embrace, life's canvas imprints true.

The Silent Guardian of the Glade

In the heart of the glade, where the shadows play,
A guardian stands watch, through night and day.
With branches outstretched, it cradles the space,
Protecting the whispers of nature's embrace.

Quiet and wise, its presence is known,
In the rustle of leaves, the calmness is grown.
Ancient as time, the stories it keeps,
In the hush of the forest, where the stillness sleeps.

Moss blankets softly, the forest floor bright,
Underneath its boughs, hearts find their light.
A sanctuary formed, where spirits can heal,
In the silent guardian, our dreams are revealed.

As seasons will change, and time passes by,
The heart of the glade continues to sigh.
Roots digging deep, like tales from the past,
A steady embrace, steadfast and vast.

So here in the stillness, we gather our thoughts,
In nature's great wisdom, solace is wrought.
The silent guardian watches the tide,
In the glade's gentle heart, we find peace inside.

Whispers of the Woodland Breeze

In shadows deep, the secrets dwell,
A gentle rustle, nature's spell.
The trees embrace the softest sigh,
As whispers float beneath the sky.

The brook hums sweet, a lullaby,
While leaves dance slow, as time slips by.
Moss-clad stones in silence rest,
Where woodland creatures know what's best.

Sunlight dapples the forest floor,
With every step, there's so much more.
A hidden world, where dreams may roam,
The woodland whispers call us home.

With every breeze, a tale unfolds,
Of ancient trees and wonders bold.
Nature's breath, a soothing balm,
In whispers, find your peace, your calm.

Echoes of Raptor's Flight

High above where eagles soar,
Their piercing calls, a wild roar.
With wings spread wide, they grace the sky,
In silent dives, their spirits fly.

Through mountain peaks, their shadows cast,
Echoes of ancestors, steadfast.
Majestic forms cut through the blue,
In every glide, a tale rings true.

The wind their ally, strong and free,
Carrying whispers, wild decree.
A dance of freedom, fierce and bright,
In echoes of the raptor's flight.

Through sunlit realms and storms so bold,
Timeless stories begging to be told.
The sky their canvas, vast and grand,
In every swoop, they make their stand.

Plumage Dreams Beneath the Pines

Beneath the pines, a soft façade,
Where colors blend, in nature's charade.
With plumage bright, the songbirds throng,
In hues that dance, where they belong.

Working magic, a painter's flair,
In every note, the world laid bare.
With every chirp, a dream takes flight,
In harmony with day and night.

The forest teems with life and cheer,
As fluttering wings draw ever near.
A tapestry of sound and sight,
In plumage dreams, pure delight.

Through leafy boughs, the sunlight streams,
Enchanting all with vibrant beams.
Under the pines, a secret stream,
Where every creature lives their dream.

Dance of the Feathered Sentinel

In twilight's glow, the guardians rise,
A sentinel with watchful eyes.
Wings of silk, gliding through the night,
In shadows deep, they take their flight.

With every flit, the world stands still,
A silent dance upon the hill.
Where whispers of the breeze align,
The feathered dancers spin and twine.

Their calls resound in hollow trees,
Awakening the sleeping breeze.
In moonlit realms, their magic weaves,
A tale of joy that never leaves.

The sky adorned with stars anew,
As night unfolds, their dreams come true.
A dance of grace, both fierce and free,
The sentinel sings in harmony.

Dancing Shadows of the Woodland Breeze

Beneath the boughs, the shadows sway,
A gentle dance at close of day.
Leaves whisper secrets in the air,
In this twilight, magic's flair.

Mossy carpets, soft and deep,
Where woodland creatures take their leap.
A symphony of night begins,
As stars peek out, the magic spins.

The cool wind carries quiet tunes,
To serenade the watchful moons.
Each flicker of the firefly,
Guides my heart as dreams draw nigh.

Crisp scents of pine fill the night,
Illuminated by silver light.
Here in the heart of nature's song,
I feel the world where I belong.

So let me linger, hold my breath,
In this realm of life and death.
Dancing shadows, wild and free,
In the woodland, I find me.

Whispers of the Skybound Hunter

High above, the eagle soars,
With keen eyes on distant shores.
His wings spread wide, a graceful arc,
In solitude, he leaves his mark.

Through clouds of white and skies of blue,
He rides the winds, a spirit true.
With every glide, stories unfold,
Of ancient legends, fierce and bold.

The sunset paints the heavens bright,
A canvas woven with golden light.
In silence, he hunts, sharp and keen,
A master of the land unseen.

The whispering winds call out his name,
In every glance, a flicker of flame.
He knows the secrets of the night,
In shadows, he dances, a ghost in flight.

So let him guide with strength profound,
The skybound hunter, grace unbound.
In his embrace, the world feels small,
A guardian watching over all.

The Echoes of Feathered Dreams

In the morning light, the songbirds sing,
A symphony that the dawn will bring.
With every chirp, a tale is spun,
Of dreams that wake with the rising sun.

The robins flit through branches green,
In every flutter, a sight unseen.
Their laughter dances on the breeze,
A melody that brings hearts to ease.

As shadows lengthen, the night takes hold,
The owls awaken, so wise and bold.
With eyes like gems, they quietly scheme,
Guardians of the twilight dream.

Through moonlit skies, their whispers glide,
In the embrace of night, they abide.
Every flutter, every flight,
Tells a story of warmth and light.

So listen close, in the starlit air,
For echoes of dreams are everywhere.
In the dance of feathers, wild and free,
Lie the secrets of eternity.

Sighs of the Timbered Refuge

In the depths of the forest, where shadows creep,
The timbered refuge holds its secrets deep.
Whispers carry on the gentle breeze,
A solace found beneath the trees.

Each rustle of leaves, a soft refrain,
As nature sighs, releasing her pain.
The trunks, like sentinels, stand so tall,
Each ring a story, a testament to all.

Moss blankets stones in emerald hues,
Where soft sunlight filters through and renews.
The air is thick with the scent of pine,
In this sacred space, the world aligns.

As twilight falls, the creatures stir,
In the hush of dusk, their hearts confer.
A dance of life, of love and strive,
Within this refuge, the wilds come alive.

So let me wander where shadows play,
In the timbered refuge, I long to stay.
With every sigh, the earth conveys,
The beauty of life in countless ways.

The Treetop Portrait of Wanderlust

In the branches high, dreams take flight,
Whispers of journeys, day and night.
Leaves dance gently, catching light,
Adventures called, a thrilling sight.

Footprints of wanderers grace the boughs,
Tales of the world, nature allows.
Colors of freedom painted bright,
In this treetop, hearts ignite.

Clouds decorate the sky's blue dress,
Mysteries wrapped in nature's caress.
A canvas of stars, the night's finesse,
Invites the lost to seek their quest.

Wind sings softly, secrets unfold,
Stories of wanderers brave and bold.
In treetops high, dreams can be sold,
A portrait of wanderlust to behold.

Roots intertwine, as do our dreams,
Binding us close with invisible seams.
With every rustle, hope redeems,
In this portrait, life gently gleams.

Wild Wings Above the Evergreen

In the stillness, wings take flight,
Across the treetops, a joyful sight.
Echoing calls beneath the light,
Wild wings soar, pure delight.

Gliding through canopies lush and wide,
Nature's marvel, a graceful glide.
Feathers sparkle, let hopes abide,
In the arms of air, spirits reside.

Evergreen whispers, ancient and wise,
Guardians of dreams beneath bright skies.
With every rustle, adventure lies,
In the heart of nature, freedom flies.

With each beat, hearts race and sing,
Life takes flight on joyous wing.
Through every turn, wild wonders bring,
The thrill of life, a wondrous thing.

Together they dance, birds in the sun,
Sharing the joy of moments spun.
In the wild, life has just begun,
Beneath the evergreens, we run.

Cerulean Dreams and Woodland Whispers

Beneath the azure sky so wide,
Woodland whispers, secrets inside.
Cerulean dreams, where hearts abide,
Nature's beauty, our humble guide.

Streams flow softly, gentle and low,
Reflecting light in a tranquil glow.
Winds tell stories, ebb and flow,
In this serene realm, love will grow.

Branches cradle the hopes we keep,
In twilight's embrace, we softly sleep.
Nature's lullaby, sweet and deep,
Cerulean dreams, for us to reap.

The moonlight weaves its silver thread,
Painting the earth where footsteps tread.
Woodland whispers, softly spread,
In the quiet night, our spirits fed.

Under stars, we find our way,
Guided by dreams at the end of day.
In this embrace, let worries sway,
In woodland whispers, we'll always stay.

A Gathering of Feathered Strangers

In the morning light, colors burst,
A gathering sweet, a joyful thirst.
Feathered strangers, they quench the first,
Of daylight's warmth, nature's trust.

Perched on branches, they greet the dawn,
Voices mingling, a melodious spawn.
In songs of love, hope is drawn,
In the vibrant air, they dance upon.

With every flutter, stories unfold,
Tales of the brave, the shy, the bold.
In the tapestry of life, we're told,
Feathered friends, treasures to hold.

Nestled together, safe and sound,
In a world where wild dreams abound.
Through laughter and songs, they are found,
In this gathering, joy resounds.

When evening falls, the flock draws near,
With whispered goodbyes, they disappear.
In hearts they linger, ever dear,
These feathered strangers, we hold near.

Passageways in the Twisted Bark

In the heart of the forest deep,
A journey through the whispers steep,
Veins of stories etched in grain,
Memories of joy and pain.

Twisted paths beneath the sky,
Embrace the roots where secrets lie,
Nature's voice, soft and low,
Guiding footsteps as they flow.

Each gnarled twist a tale to share,
Echoes linger in the air,
Life's transition, swift and stark,
Exploring just beyond the dark.

Hidden realms in softest hues,
Mossy carpets, earthy views,
Through the bark, life intertwines,
A tapestry of life's designs.

Passageways in the twisted bark,
Invite the dreamers, light the dark,
In the stillness, truth will gleam,
Awakening the heart's own dream.

Flutters of Light in the Canopied Calm

Through the leaves, a gentle dance,
Sunbeams weave, a fleeting glance,
Fluttering whispers in the air,
A soft repose, a moment rare.

In the stillness, shadows play,
Nature's lullaby leads the way,
Golden rays on emerald green,
A radiant glow, a tranquil scene.

The canopy holds stories bright,
Flutters of joy in the light,
Caught in time, a breath so sweet,
Where earth and sky blissfully meet.

With every flitter, spirits rise,
Moments captured, love supplies,
Breath of nature, short yet deep,
In the calm, our souls shall seep.

Flutters of light, a soft embrace,
In this sanctuary, find your place,
Where time is still, a gentle balm,
In the canopied, peaceful calm.

Sentinel Shadows on Dappled Ground

Under the shade, secrets confide,
Sentinel shadows, side by side,
Guardians of the ancient lore,
Time stands still on forest floor.

Dappled sunlight paints the scene,
Nature's quilt in hues serene,
Every shadow tells a tale,
Quiet whispers fill the vale.

Footsteps echo on the trail,
Interwoven in the gale,
Where the trees stand, wise and grand,
Earth and sky at their command.

Beneath the boughs where dreams reside,
Sheltering hopes, the stars abide,
Sentinels watch, steadfast and true,
In their embrace, we renew.

Sentinel shadows, time stands still,
In the heart of woods, find your will,
On dappled ground, the world unfolds,
In silent stories, life's truth holds.

Branches Hold Their Secrets

High above, the branches weave,
Holding tales that none believe,
In their crooks, the whispers cling,
Ancient songs the leaves still sing.

Through each bough, the stories flow,
Silent witnesses to all below,
Twisting tales from dusk till dawn,
Under the moon, where dreams are drawn.

Nestled close, where shadows blend,
Where beginnings meet their end,
Branches hold a sacred space,
In every curve, a life embraced.

Overhead, the sky paints fast,
Moments captured, forever cast,
Tales of heartache, love, and loss,
In the branches, we count the cost.

Branches hold their secrets tight,
In the day and in the night,
With every rustle, gently we find,
The echoes of the past combined.

Flickers of Flight in the Sunlight

Birds dance high in azure skies,
Soft whispers of gentle sighs,
Wings spread wide with dreams so bright,
Caught in beams of golden light.

Flickers dash through swaying trees,
Carried forth by warm, sweet breeze,
Nature calls in radiant hues,
Where every moment feels like news.

Sunlight glimmers on river streams,
Crafting shadows, weaving dreams,
Here, the world starts to ignite,
With flickers of flight in daylight.

Among the clouds, their songs take flight,
Creating art, pure delight,
In a realm of endless height,
Where all hearts blend, pure and light.

As day descends, the colors blend,
The evening hush, a faithful friend,
With every twilight's soft embrace,
New flickers form, time starts to race.

Beneath the Pine's Embrace

Beneath the pine, where shadows play,
Whispers of nature softly sway,
Roots entwined in earth's embrace,
A sacred, calm, and peaceful space.

Sunlight pierces through the leaves,
Nature's song, the heart believes,
Swaying branches, gentle sighs,
Underneath the watchful skies.

Mossy blankets on the ground,
In this haven, peace is found,
A refuge from the busy world,
As time unfurls, dreams are curled.

The scent of pine, a sweet release,
In every breath, a spark of peace,
Beneath the boughs, the heart can race,
Finding joy in nature's grace.

As twilight lingers, stars appear,
In this moment, all is clear,
Wrapped in night's soft, cool embrace,
Beneath the pine, we find our place.

Whispers of a Painted Sky

Whispers swirl in shades of blue,
As day surrenders, magic brews,
Strokes of red and gold combine,
To paint a canvas, by design.

Clouds transform in fiery dance,
Each hue, a dream ignited chance,
Beneath this vast, transforming dome,
The heart finds peace, to wander home.

As sunlight fades, the stars awake,
Soft glimmers on the water's lake,
Reflections catch the fleeting light,
Each moment, a pure delight.

In the quiet of twilight's kiss,
Every shadow brings forth bliss,
Whispers echo, secrets shared,
In painted skies, all hearts bared.

With every dusk, new tales are spun,
In the twilight, we become one,
A symphony of colors bright,
Lost in whispers of the night.

Watchful Eyes and Woven Tales

In the forest where shadows blend,
Watchful eyes seem to suspend,
Every rustle, every breeze,
Holds a story, whispers tease.

Woven tales of ancient lore,
Echo through the woodland floor,
In the bark, in the streams that flow,
Every secret starts to grow.

Creatures lurking, silent dance,
In their gaze, a fleeting chance,
A curious heart must just explore,
What secrets lay behind each door.

Underneath the moon's soft glow,
Every shadow starts to flow,
Tales unfold, like timeless dreams,
Enchanting all with whispered themes.

As night deepens, one might find,
The woven tales that bind the kind,
In watchful eyes, there's wisdom shared,
In silent hearts, all dreams laid bare.

Nature's Palette on the Wooden Plank

Colors splash on leaves of green,
A canvas born from sunbeam's sheen.
Rustling whispers, winds entwine,
Nature's art, forever divine.

Brushstrokes of dusk, hues ablaze,
In twilight's grip, the world will gaze.
Golden rays on water gleam,
Reflecting life, a soothing dream.

Gentle rains, a soft caress,
Murmurs of growth, nature's finesse.
Petals dance, a vibrant swirl,
A symphony of life unfurl.

In every shadow, stories hide,
A journey painted, side by side.
Beneath the boughs, secrets linger,
Nature's touch, a tender singer.

So let the colors sing aloud,
In harmony, beneath the cloud.
For on this plank, life takes its stand,
Nature's palette, forever grand.

The Quiet Dance of the Resilient Heart

In silence blooms a steadfast grace,
Beating softly, this sacred space.
With every pulse, a tale unfolds,
Of battles fought and dreams retold.

Through stormy nights and brightening dawn,
It whispers courage, never withdrawn.
A gentle sway, a rhythmic flow,
The heart persists, this truth we know.

In shadows cast, it finds its light,
A quiet dance, a soulful flight.
With every thump, a promise made,
In depths of trials, hope won't fade.

So let it beat, this vibrant sound,
A legacy that knows no bound.
Against the odds, it finds its way,
The resilient heart, forever sway.

Embrace the quiet, feel it near,
This dance of life, a rhythm clear.
For in each pulse, strength intertwines,
The heart, an echo that always shines.

Echoes of the Wild in the Stillness

In quiet woods, a secret sigh,
Where shadows blend and dreams float by.
The wild calls out, a distant tune,
In whispers soft beneath the moon.

Crickets chirp and owls take flight,
Under the watch of starlit night.
Every rustle, a story told,
Of nature's magic, brave and bold.

Among the pines, a gentle breeze,
Carries echoes that plant the seeds.
Of ancient tales and playful sprites,
Awake the echoes, ignite the sights.

In stillness lie the truths that bind,
A sacred peace, a loving mind.
Here the wild and calm converge,
Nature's pulse begins to surge.

So listen close, and breathe it in,
The wild's embrace, where life begins.
In every echo, hear the call,
For in the stillness, we find it all.

Serenade in a Pine-Scented Haven

Beneath the boughs, a solace found,
Where whispers weave a magic sound.
The pine trees sway in rhythmic grace,
Embracing all in nature's space.

A gentle song floats on the air,
Fresh aromas, like a prayer.
In every breeze, the heart takes flight,
A serenade to the starry night.

Among the needles, dreams take form,
Creating warmth, a refuge warm.
Each note a hug, each breath a kiss,
This pine-scented world, a perfect bliss.

When shadows fall, and stillness reigns,
The melody of life remains.
In whispered tones, the forest speaks,
In every heartbeat, joy it seeks.

So rest your soul, let worries cease,
In nature's arms, you find your peace.
For in this haven, dreams align,
A serenade, forever entwined.

Feathers in the Twilight Glint

In the dusk, they softly gleam,
Whispers of a fading dream.
Shadows dance upon the earth,
Embers glow, a gentle birth.

A flutter hints of wings above,
Nature wraps us in its love.
Each flap tells a hidden tale,
Of journeys that will not unveil.

Silhouettes against the glow,
Feathered friends in twilight's flow.
With every breeze, they take flight,
Leaving trails of soft twilight.

Beneath the arch of fading light,
Silent creatures take their flight.
In the hush, secrets remain,
Held close within the quiet grain.

As stars blink in the velvet sky,
Whispers of the night draw nigh.
Feathers drift through the cool night air,
Carrying dreams beyond compare.

The Perch of Nature's Watcher

Upon the branch so high and proud,
Silent guardian, yet unbowed.
Eyes so keen, they pierce the veil,
Listening to the timeless tale.

Rustling leaves, they stir the breeze,
Traces of the roaming bees.
Every chirp, a fleeting song,
Nature's chorus, ever strong.

From this perch, all life unfolds,
Stories of the brave and bold.
In the sun's warm, golden glow,
Beauty in the ebb and flow.

Watching as the seasons change,
Each moment, both wild and strange.
Time stands still in this sweet place,
Nature holds its soft embrace.

So here it rests, the watcher's state,
Guarding dreams and hearts so great.
In the quiet of fading light,
Essence of the day takes flight.

Breezy Tales from the Forest Edge

Where the green meets azure skies,
Gentle whispers, nature sighs.
Breezes carry tales untold,
In each leaf, in every fold.

Footprints barely mark the ground,
Echoes in the air resound.
From the thicket, laughter flies,
Chirping pals in joyous ties.

Stories weave through branches bare,
Lifted, cast upon the air.
With each gust, the forest sways,
In the dance of winding ways.

Sunbeams filter, warmth cascades,
In the hush, the magic fades.
But the breeze, it carries on,
Weaving threads 'til break of dawn.

Listen close, the voices play,
Nature's tune throughout the day.
In the rustle, joy is found,
Breezy tales, forever bound.

Pinecone Memories in Flight

Beneath the boughs where shadows lie,
Pinecones fall from branches high.
Each a keeper of the past,
Memories made, forever cast.

Scattered seeds of nature's grace,
In the forest's warm embrace.
With each breeze, they spin and dance,
Carrying hopes, a second chance.

Whispered dreams in muted tones,
Rustling softly among the stones.
Time-worn tales of seasons gone,
In their hearts, they linger on.

As the skies begin to fade,
Hope unfolds in every shade.
Pinecone wishes take to flight,
Guided by the stars so bright.

With every journey, new and bold,
Secrets of the woods retold.
In the twilight's soft embrace,
Pinecone memories find their place.

Skies Painted by Small Wings

In twilight's glow, they soar high,
A canvas where the larks fly by.
Whispers of wings, soft and sweet,
They dance in air, where daylight meets.

The colors blend, a vibrant hue,
As they weave dreams of sky so blue.
Nature's brush, with gentle ease,
Creates a world that aims to please.

With every flit, a tale is spun,
Of fleeting moments kissed by sun.
The skies, alive, their joy displayed,
By small wings' flights, a serenade.

In fading light, a hush descends,
While twilight draws, the day soon ends.
But echoes of their songs remain,
In hearts that felt their sweet refrain.

So let us gaze at evening's stage,
Where small wings dance in ageless page.
For in their flight, we find our song,
In skies where brief moments belong.

The Pines Remember Their Visitors

In shadows tall, the pines stand firm,
Guardians of secrets, timeless and warm.
They whisper tales of those who've walked,
In hushed tones, the forest talked.

Each bough, a witness, each needle, a tear,
To laughter and tears from those held dear.
The scent of earth, the crunch of leaves,
Echo the stories that nature weaves.

From gentle souls to woeful cries,
The pines remember beneath the skies.
A rustle of branches, a breeze that sighs,
Recalls the history, where time flies.

In winter's chill or summer's grace,
Visitors come to find their place.
With each new step, a memory forms,
As pines embrace all seasons' storms.

Their roots entwined with the earth they share,
Holding the stories, a bond so rare.
From child's laughter to lovers' sighs,
The pines, in silence, hold all goodbyes.

As twilight paints the world in gold,
They stand steadfast, their tales retold.
In every breeze, remember this truth:
The pines endure, they hold our youth.

Colors of Dawn and Feathered Greetings

The dawn breaks softly, a painted sky,
With hues that beckon the day to fly.
Robins chirp, with vibrant calls,
As morning's song through silence falls.

Each feathered friend, a brush of light,
In colors bold, they take their flight.
The world awakens, filled with chance,
As nature's creatures begin to dance.

The golden rays kiss every leaf,
Bringing life to the still and brief.
And in this moment, hope ignites,
A tapestry of joyful sights.

Where shadows fade and warmth appears,
The feathered greetings melt our fears.
In every song, a promise gleams,
Colors of dawn, in waking dreams.

As sun ascends to claim its throne,
We find our place, no longer alone.
For in this day, with spirits high,
We embrace the beauty of the sky.

Breaths of Pine and Feathers' Grace

In forest deep where silence reigns,
The pine trees breathe with gentle strains.
Each whisper sways in time and space,
With nature's pulse, a soft embrace.

The feathers float on warm spring air,
As creatures roam with hearts laid bare.
In every flutter, life reveals,
The grace embedded in all it feels.

Sunlight dapples 'neath the boughs,
A sacred moment, a quiet vow.
The world pauses, as if to hear,
The harmony that draws us near.

With every breath, the pines exhale,
Stories woven through winds' soft trail.
Feathers gather in endless flight,
Bringing the dawn to banish night.

Together they rise, in peace and grace,
Nature's tableau, a warm embrace.
In breaths of pine and songs so sweet,
The dance of life, where all dreams meet.

Secrets of the Timbered Threshold

Whispers dwell in aged wood,
Where roots entwine in silent broods.
Each beam tells tales of storms and sun,
A realm where time and essence run.

Moss blankets stones in emerald dreams,
While shadows dance in sunlit beams.
Footsteps echo on forest's floor,
In nature's heart, we seek for more.

Beneath the boughs, a secret lies,
In rustling leaves, the heart complies.
Ancient spirits watch and wait,
Guiding us to woods of fate.

In twilight's glow, the secrets blend,
A whispered truth the trees recommend.
Branches cradle hopes and fears,
Telling stories through the years.

With every rustle, life unfolds,
Tales of wonders yet untold.
Embrace the woods, their sacred flow,
For timbered thresholds brightly glow.

Shadows on the Needle-Covered Floor

The forest floor in hushed repose,
A tapestry where silence grows.
Shadows stretch, then softly creep,
To cradle secrets safe in sleep.

Needles fall like whispered sighs,
As twilight paints the dusky skies.
Footfalls muted, spirits near,
Awakening the night's quiet cheer.

Echoes swirl in twilight's breath,
Dancing softly with the depth.
A world alive with whispered lore,
Beneath the trees, forevermore.

Crickets sing a hallowed song,
Where shadows weave and dreams belong.
In this realm of hush and grace,
Nature's pulse, a warm embrace.

And so we wander, hearts in tow,
Through needle paths where breezes blow.
In every shadow, life is bound,
A tranquil peace in nature found.

Glimpses of the Skyward Hunter

High above, the falcon flies,
With keen gaze on the endless skies.
Dancing 'round on currents strong,
A master where the winds belong.

Feathers trace a path so bold,
In twilight's hush, a sight to behold.
With every beat, the heavens call,
Through endless heights, the hunter sprawls.

A flash of wings, a critical dive,
In the wild dance, the thrill of life.
With nimble grace, the air it cleaves,
For every heartbeat, purpose weaves.

Beneath the clouds, a world so wide,
The hunter soars with effortless pride.
Through sunlit realms, it seeks its claim,
In sacred skies, it plays the game.

And as the dusk begins to fade,
A hush befalls the evening glade.
In dreams of flight, we find our worth,
Glimpses of freedom on this earth.

Song of the Rustic Aviary

In the eaves, the sparrows sing,
With happiness that spring will bring.
Nestled close, a harmony,
Echoes of sweet simplicity.

Wings that flutter, soft and light,
Fill the air with sheer delight.
Each note a tale from branch to branch,
A melodic world in joyous dance.

Through garden blooms, their laughter weaves,
A rustic charm that never leaves.
The dawn awakens songs anew,
In rustling leaves, a sacred view.

As starlit nights embrace the day,
The songs of dusk come out to play.
With owls that hoot and crickets strum,
An evening waltz of all who hum.

So raise your voice, let echoes soar,
Join the choir forevermore.
In every tweet, a heart obeys,
In rustic aviary, we find our ways.

A Rustic Haven on Nature's Edge

In valleys deep, where whispers flow,
The wildflowers bloom, in colors aglow.
Old stones and branches weave their tale,
In a rustic haven, where spirits sail.

The sun dips low, casting golden light,
While shadows dance in the soft twilight.
Birds serenade with a joyful song,
In this tranquil place, where hearts belong.

A gentle breeze stirs the lush green leaves,
Carrying secrets that nature weaves.
Amidst the oak and the willow's grace,
Lies a calm refuge, a sacred space.

Night falls softly, a silken veil,
Crickets play, and stars unveil.
The moonlight kisses the tranquil pond,
In this haven, of which we're so fond.

With dawn, the world wakes anew,
Painting the sky in vibrant hue.
Each moment here, pure and divine,
In this rustic charm, we intertwine.

Beneath Turquoise and Cedar

Beneath the cedar, shadows fall,
Where turquoise waters gently call.
Ripples dance in the sunlight's glow,
Whispers of secrets in breezes blow.

The air is sweet with pine's embrace,
In this quiet, cherished place.
Nature sings a soothing song,
In the heart of woods, where we belong.

Dappled sunlight through branches streams,
Awakens the forest, stirs our dreams.
A tapestry woven of leaf and sky,
In this sacred space, we learn to fly.

In cool shade, the earth feels blessed,
Wrapped in nature's warm caress.
Each moment spent, a gift so rare,
A memory held in the summer air.

As twilight beckons, the stars appear,
Echoes of laughter, music we hear.
Together we stand, in awe of this scene,
Beneath turquoise skies, where life is serene.

Ballet of Shadows on Old Wood

On old wood floors, shadows sway,
In a subtle ballet, they play.
Each crack and creak tells a tale,
Of moments past, where dreams prevail.

The sunlight streams through windows wide,
Casting patterns, a gentle guide.
Here in the stillness, time stands still,
In this dance of shadows, hearts are filled.

A whiff of musk, of ages gone,
The lingering scent of history's song.
Each brush of light, a lover's touch,
In this old world, we cherish so much.

The evening comes with a soft embrace,
Bringing whispers of night's grace.
We sway to the rhythm of dreams anew,
On old wood floors, where love shines through.

As stars emerge in the deepening blue,
The shadows waltz with the night so true.
In this ballet of old wood and light,
We find our peace by the moon's soft sight.

Harmony in Feathers and Bark

In the forest vast, a symphony thrives,
With whispers of trees and the flutter of lives.
Feathers in flight, a delicate dance,
Among ancient bark, they take their chance.

The songs of the birds, sweet and clear,
Echo the laughter of nature near.
Rustling leaves join in the refrain,
A harmony born from sunshine and rain.

Each creature small plays its part,
In the grand design, a work of art.
Nature's canvas, both wild and free,
A tapestry rich, for all to see.

As the sun sets low, the world grows dim,
The nightingale sings, a lullaby hymn.
Together they weave a tale so bright,
Of harmony found in the heart of night.

With dawn approaching, the world awakes,
In this sacred space, where magic takes.
Feathers and bark, in unity thrive,
In nature's embrace, we come alive.

www.ingramcontent.com/pod-product-compliance
Ingram Content Group UK Ltd.
Pitfield, Milton Keynes, MK11 3LW, UK
UKHW021532210125
4208UKWH00025B/587

9 781805 596080